N. T. WRIGHT
FOR EVERYONE
BIBLE STUDY GUIDES

# COLOSSIANS & PHILEMON

## 8 STUDIES FOR INDIVIDUALS AND GROUPS

# N. T. WRIGHT

## WITH DALE & SANDY LARSEN

IVP Connect
An imprint of InterVarsity Press
Downers Grove, Illinois

*InterVarsity Press*
*P.O. Box 1400, Downers Grove, IL 60515-1426*
*World Wide Web: www.ivpress.com*
*E-mail: email@ivpress.com*

*InterVarsity Press® is the book-publishing division of InterVarsity Christian Fellowship/USA®, a movement of students and faculty active on campus at hundreds of universities, colleges and schools of nursing in the United States of America, and a member movement of the International Fellowship of Evangelical Students. For information about local and regional activities, write Public Relations Dept., InterVarsity Christian Fellowship/USA, 6400 Schroeder Rd., P.O. Box 7895, Madison, WI 53707-7895, or visit the IVCF website at <www.intervarsity.org>.*

*Cover design: Cindy Kiple*
*Cover image: jessekarjalainen/iStockphoto*

*ISBN 978-0-8308-2192-1*

*Printed in the United States of America* ∞

| P | 18 | 17 | 16 | 15 | 14 | 13 | 12 | 11 | 10 | 9 | 8 | 7 | 6 | 5 | 4 | 3 | 2 | 1 |
|---|----|----|----|----|----|----|----|----|----|---|---|---|---|---|---|---|---|---|
| Y | 24 | 23 | 22 | 21 | 20 | 19 | 18 | 17 | 16 | 15 | 14 | 13 | 12 | 11 | 10 | 09 | | | |

# CONTENTS

# GETTING THE MOST
# OUT OF COLOSSIANS
# AND PHILEMON

We watched, holding our breath, as the mother duck left the pond at the head of her brood.

There were seven ducklings in all: four black ones and three yellow ones. They were lively and squeaky, scuttling to and fro. For days they had swum about with their mother in the little pond. Now it was time for her to take them to the nearby lake.

This meant danger. To get there they had to cross a main road and make their way through a park where dogs, cats, larger birds and several other predators would be watching. Fortunately, in this city at least, local residents are prepared for this moment and make sure that traffic comes to a stop to let the little procession pass through. They reached their destination safely. But we were left marveling at the mother's apparent calm confidence as she led her little family through potential hazards and on to the larger world where she would then bring them up to maturity.

Paul must often have felt like a mother duck. Here he was writing to a little church in Colossae, a town about a hundred miles inland on the banks of the river Lycus in the southeast of what is now Turkey. The church was just starting up, full of energy and enthusiasm but hardly yet aware of the great dangers and problems that were to be faced.

Now as he writes this letter to the Colossians, he is in prison, most likely in Ephesus, and he can't even be with them in person to guide them and teach them. The mother duck has to rely on instinct—her own, and that of her recently born babies—to see them through. But ordinary human instinct alone won't get the young church through to maturity. Human instincts are important, but they remain earthbound. When people become Christians, God implants into them a new sense of his presence and love, his guiding and strengthening. This sense needs nurturing and developing. New Christians need to understand what's happening to them, and how they must cooperate with the divine life that's gently begun to work in them.

It's probable that the short letter to Philemon was on its way to Colossae at the same time, since we note that the letter to the Colossians includes a mention of Philemon's slave, Onesiumus (Colossians 4:9). Onesimus was going back to Colossae, and to Philemon's household, along with Tychicus, to whom Paul is entrusting the letter we are now reading. (For more on these two letters, also see my *Paul for Everyone: The Prison Letters* published by SPCK and Westminster John Knox. This guide is based on that book and has been prepared with the help of Dale and Sandy Larsen, for which I am grateful. An additional resource you can consult is my Tyndale New Testament Commentary, *Colossians & Philemon*, from InterVarsity Press.)

Paul's own personal circumstances make this letter especially poignant, and give us a portrait of a man facing huge difficulties and hardships and coming through with his faith and hope unscathed. But what he has to say to the young church is even more impressive. Already, within thirty years of Jesus' death and resurrection, Paul has worked out a wonderful, many-colored picture of what Jesus achieved, of God's worldwide plan, and of how it all works out in the lives of ordinary people—people like you and me.

## SUGGESTIONS FOR INDIVIDUAL STUDY

1.  As you begin each study, pray that God will speak to you through his Word.

2. Read the introduction to the study and respond to the "Open" question that follows it. This is designed to help you get into the theme of the study.

3. Read and reread the Bible passage to be studied. Each study is designed to help you consider the meaning of the passage in its context. The commentary and questions in this guide are based on my own translation of each passage found in the companion volume to this guide in the For Everyone series on the New Testament (published by SPCK and Westminster John Knox).

4. Write your answers to the questions in the spaces provided or in a personal journal. Each study includes three types of questions: observation questions, which ask about the basic facts in the passage; interpretation questions, which delve into the meaning of the passage; and application questions, which help you discover the implications of the text for growing in Christ. Writing out your responses can bring clarity and deeper understanding of yourself and of God's Word.

5. Each session features selected comments from the For Everyone series. These notes provide further biblical and cultural background and contextual information. They are designed not to answer the questions for you but to help you along as you study the Bible for yourself. For even more reflections on each passage, you may wish to have on hand a copy of the companion volume from the For Everyone series as you work through this study guide.

6. Use the guidelines in the "Pray" section to focus on God, thanking him for what you have learned and praying about the applications that have come to mind.

## SUGGESTIONS FOR GROUP MEMBERS

1. Come to the study prepared. Follow the suggestions for individual study mentioned above. You will find that careful preparation will greatly enrich your time spent in group discussion.

2. Be willing to participate in the discussion. The leader of your group

will not be lecturing. Instead, she or he will be asking the questions found in this guide and encouraging the members of the group to discuss what they have learned.

3. Stick to the topic being discussed. These studies focus on a particular passage of Scripture. Only rarely should you refer to other portions of the Bible or outside sources. This allows for everyone to participate on equal ground and for in-depth study.

4. Be sensitive to the other members of the group. Listen attentively when they describe what they have learned. You may be surprised by their insights! Each question assumes a variety of answers. Many questions do not have "right" answers, particularly questions that aim at meaning or application. Instead the questions push us to explore the passage more thoroughly.

   When possible, link what you say to the comments of others. Also, be affirming whenever you can. This will encourage some of the more hesitant members of the group to participate.

5. Be careful not to dominate the discussion. We are sometimes so eager to express our thoughts that we leave too little opportunity for others to respond. By all means participate! But allow others to also.

6. Expect God to teach you through the passage being discussed and through the other members of the group. Pray that you will have an enjoyable and profitable time together, but also that as a result of the study you will find ways that you can take action individually and/ or as a group.

7. It will be helpful for groups to follow a few basic guidelines. These guidelines, which you may wish to adapt to your situation, should be read at the beginning of the first session.

   • Anything said in the group is considered confidential and will not be discussed outside the group unless specific permission is given to do so.

   • We will provide time for each person present to talk if he or she feels comfortable doing so.

- We will talk about ourselves and our own situations, avoiding conversation about other people.

- We will listen attentively to each other.

- We will be very cautious about giving advice.

Additional suggestions for the group leader can be found at the back of the guide.

# THE FRUIT OF THE GOSPEL

*Colossians 1:1-14*

Wh  en Susan bought the house, there wasn't much growing in the garden. It was a depressing sight. Then a friend came to visit and brought some seeds. They were special, he said, not what you'd expect. Once you'd sown them and watered them, plants would grow vigorously and would quickly cover a large area with beautiful flowers. That wasn't all. Hidden under the leaves would be a delicious fruit. When the fruit appeared and ripened, you'd know the plants had come to stay. Within a week or two Susan's garden was transformed. She telephoned her friend. What on earth was this new plant? Ah, he said, it's new. It's transforming gardens everywhere. You're part of a whole new world.

Now I don't think there really is a plant like that. I tell the story because Paul has such a scene in mind as he starts the short letter to the Christians in Colossae. Paul is delighted that the wonderful new plant of the gospel has been planted in Colossae and that it's bearing fruit and growing, as indeed it is doing in the rest of the world.

## OPEN

Think of a time when you saw someone's life radically change for the better. How did you react to the change? What did you think and say about that person? to that person?

## STUDY

1. *Read Colossians 1:1-14.* Since Paul himself was the one who brought the "plant" of the gospel to this part of the world, he wants them to know that he's thanking God that it's taking root with them, and he wants to tell them how to nurture it and help it to bear more fruit. The fruit, in fact, has already begun to appear, and it's interesting to see that this is what Paul focuses on when he tells them how he heard about the new church coming into being.

   What qualities does Paul see in the lives of the Colossians that indicate the gospel is bearing fruit in their lives?

2. How do those qualities reflect the good news of Jesus Christ?

   Paul assumes an unspoken contrast here. The behavior which marks out so much of the world—lust, anger, lies and so on, which split up families and communities—is being replaced by kindness, gentleness, forgiveness and an acceptance of one another as members of the same family, even where there were major differences of race, background and culture. This, as far as Paul is concerned, is the true sign of God at work, and he is thrilled and grateful to hear about it.

3.  The seed which was planted in Colossae was what Paul describes as
    "the word of truth, the gospel" (v. 5). This word is powerful. When it
    is spoken, God himself works through it, spreading the plant of new
    life, color, fragrance and fruit in every place.

    To what extent would you say the fruit of "the word of truth, the
    gospel" is evident in your own life?

4.  Looking at this passage, what would be the reasons for a lack of
    spiritual fruit?

    The gospel doesn't just produce a new religious experience for
    those who might like such a thing. It brings about something much
    greater: nothing less than a new creation. When people become
    Christians, God implants into them a new sense of his presence and
    love, his guiding and strengthening. This sense needs nurturing and
    developing. New Christians need to understand what's happening
    to them and how they must cooperate with the divine life that has
    gently begun to work in them. Paul, in prison, can help this process
    in two ways: by writing, as he is doing, but supremely by prayer.

5.  Whether you're a new Christian yourself, needing to grow in the
    faith, or a Christian leader, wanting to nurture those in your care,
    Paul's prayer for the new church in Colossae provides a wonderful
    pattern (vv. 9-12). What does Paul pray concerning the will of God
    (vv. 9-10)?

6.  Why is understanding God's will important for spiritual growth?

7.  What does Paul specifically pray for the Christians in Colossae (vv. 11-12)?

8.  Look over Paul's prayer in verses 9-12. What would it mean for someone to pray these things for you? Think of specific areas where you need those prayers.

9.  Who do you know that needs your prayers modeled on verses 9-12?

10. The climax of Paul's prayer is that the young Christians will learn the art of thanksgiving. What Paul most wants to see growing in the church, as a sign of healthy Christian life on the way to maturity, is gratitude to God for the extraordinary things he's done in Jesus and the remarkable things he is continuing to do in the world and in their lives. Spontaneous gratitude of this kind is a sign that they are coming to know and love the true God.

    When, why and how do you most frequently thank God?

## PRAY

Pray that what Paul heard about the Colossians will also be said of you and your Christian fellowship. Pray that you will be marked by wisdom, love, faith, hope and a spirit of thanksgiving.

# CHRIST SUPREME

*Colossians 1:15-29*

If there is somebody sitting in the next room, I can't see them because there's a wall in the way. But if there is a mirror out in the hallway, I may be able to look out of my door and see, in the mirror, the mirror-image of the person in the next room. In the same way, Jesus is the mirror-image of the God who is there but who we normally can't see. We may be aware of his presence; many people, many religions, many systems of philosophy have admitted that there is "something or somebody there." But with Jesus we find ourselves looking at the true God himself.

The great thing is that the more we look at Jesus, the more we realize that the true God is the God of utter self-giving love. That's why the poem of Colossians 1:15-20 comes right after Paul's prayer that the Colossians will learn how to be grateful to God. When you realize that Jesus reveals who God is, gratitude is the first and most appropriate reaction.

## OPEN

What does it mean to be the *head* of something? What do you expect from someone who is designated the *head*?

More responsibility, in charge,
at them ?¿

## STUDY

1. *Read Colossians 1:15-20.* This passage is actually a poem, one of the very earliest Christian poems ever written. Paul wrote it (or, if the poem was originally written by someone else, quoted it) to show the Colossians the center of Christianity. It isn't simply about a particular way of being religious. It isn't about a particular system for how to be saved here or hereafter. It isn't simply a different way of holiness. Christianity is about Jesus Christ.

   How would you sum up what the poem reveals about Christ?

   *Everything is about Him & for Him.*

2. How was—and is—Jesus supreme in creation (vv. 15-17)? .

   *Was before & in.          Made for him
   the head of the church*

3. How was—and is—Jesus supreme in redemption (vv. 18-20)?

   *We are reconciled through Him*

Jesus Christ, says the poem boldly, is the one through whom and for whom the whole creation was made in the first place. When the lavish and generous beauty of the world makes you catch your breath, remember that it is like that because of Jesus. But it's also full of ugliness and evil, summed up in death itself. That wasn't the original intention, and the living God has now acted to heal the world of the wickedness and corruption which have so radically infected it. He has done so through the same one through whom it was made in the first place. The Jesus through whom the world was made is the same

Jesus through whom the world has now been redeemed. He is the firstborn of all creation *and* the firstborn from the dead.

4. If we are to grow as Christians, increasing in wisdom, power, patience and thanksgiving, we need to know above all what the Colossians needed to know: *the centrality and supremacy of Jesus Christ.*

What are the implications of the centrality and supremacy of Christ for your home and family life? for your work and/or volunteer life? or for your church or your life as a citizen?

*to realize that He is in control & we can't escape that.*

5. *Read Colossians 1:21-29.* If you have ever gotten lost in a large shopping mall, you know how reassuring it is to find a map with a spot labeled "You Are Here." Paul knows that the poem he set forth in verses 15-20 was quite overpowering. Many Christians might read it and think, *Well, that sounds impressive, but what's in it for me?* So Paul brings things into focus. Verses 21-23 might be headed "You Are Here." If the poem is like a map of the entire cosmos, the whole story of creation and redemption, these verses indicate where the ordinary Christian is located on the map.

How do you respond to the idea that you are in God's presence "holy, blameless and without any accusation" (v. 22)?

*So thankful because I know I'm not*

6. What are one or two ways in which your life is different since you were changed from being alienated from God to being reconciled through Christ's death (vv. 21-22)? *hard for me to remember life w/out reconciliation?*

If you do not feel you have experienced this reconciliation, what hope do you find in verses 21-23?

The purposes of God were entrusted to Israel, the promise-bearing people. People living in Colossae, like people in most other places in the world, were outside Israel. They were Gentiles, worshiping idols rather than the one true God, ignorant both of God's saving purposes and of how they themselves could share in the benefits of those purposes. But now the Colossians find themselves inside. They are on the map, part of the action.

The Colossians—and all of us who have come into the family of God from outside—are like people who have been on the street outside a royal palace, and who have suddenly been told they are invited in to appear before the king. Or, if you prefer, they are like people who have been outside the temple in Jerusalem, impure, unfit to appear in the presence of God. Now, suddenly, they have been told they are summoned in, indeed, welcomed in. What has happened to make them ready for the presence of this king, this God, is the death of King Jesus.

7.  What does Paul mean by *faith* in Colossians 1:4 and 23?

> holding onto the beliefs in
> Christ; knowing + believing Jesus

Paul says that the gospel was announced not just to a small number of men and women in a few small parts of the Mediterranean world—but to "every creature under heaven." What can he mean? He can only mean that when Jesus of Nazareth rose from the dead, as king and Lord of the world, a kind of spiritual shock wave ran right through the entire cosmos. This was a new kind of event. Nobody had ever gone down into death before and come up the other side. God's new creation had begun: Jesus is, as the poem had said (v. 18), the beginning, the firstborn from the dead, and now he is bringing to birth the reconciliation and renewal of all things in heaven and on earth.

8. What was the source of Paul's joy (vv. 24-25)?

*Ministering, sharing the gospel whatever the cost.*

Paul sees his own sufferings as part of what he calls Christ's "afflictions" (v. 24). This is not to be seen as an *addition* to Christ's own suffering; rather, it is to be seen as an *extension* of it. Paul made the remarkable statement that he was, as I translate verse 24, "having a celebration—a celebration of my sufferings."

9. Paul twice refers to a *mystery* (vv. 26-27). Where and how has it been revealed? *through Jesus Christ in you*

10. The risen life of Christ is the source of the church's hope. Every individual Christian has this hope within his or her own self. The reason is simple: Jesus the Messiah, the king, lives by his spirit within each one. How have you experienced "the king, living within you as the hope of glory" (v. 27)?

11. Verses 28-29 are full of active exertion. What keeps them from
    sounding like drudgery? *good to know, works w/*
    *His energy, not mine*

12. Paul can't stop talking about King Jesus. The church in Colossae has
    never met Paul, but he says in verses 28-29 that if they want to know
    what he spends most of his time doing, it is this: he announces Jesus
    as king and Lord. And he does it with the aim of bringing as many as
    possible to mature Christian living "in the king," "in Christ." How
    has your view of Christ been confirmed or enriched by this study?

### PRAY

Offer prayers of praise and submission to Christ, *the image of the invisible God, the firstborn over all creation, the firstborn from the dead, the
head of his body the church.*

# GOD'S TREASURE REVEALED

*Colossians 2:1-7*

In many adventure stories such as Robert Louis Stevenson's *Treasure Island*, the plot hinges on the discovery of an ancient map or chart. The people who have found it realize that, if only they could understand and follow it, it would lead them to buried treasure that had been hidden for many years, perhaps centuries. They would be rich beyond their wildest imagination.

Paul has spoken of God's secret plan, a plan that has lain hidden, like a map in a locked and dusty cupboard, for ages and generations. Now, quite suddenly, it has come to light in the events concerning Jesus the Messiah. Paul is in possession of the map and is inviting as many people as possible to come with him to find the treasure.

## OPEN

What is the most valuable thing you have ever found? What did you do with what you found? Who did you tell?

*not sure...*

## STUDY

1. *Read Colossians 2:1-7.* Paul tells the Colossians plainly what the treasure is, what dangers they will face as they try to make it their own and which route they must take to get to it. After what Paul has already said, we shouldn't be surprised that his theme all through is King Jesus, King Jesus, King Jesus. He is the secret plan; he is the treasure; he is the one "in whom" they will be able to ward off danger; he is the one "in whom" they must find their way to the goal.

From verses 1-5, sum up Paul's joys and concerns for the Colossians.

*excited to see them experience Jesus*
*concerned people will question*

2. On the "map" of your life what were the signposts along the way that led you to Christ?

*• aunts baptism*
*• church*
*• Sunday school teachers*
*• parents*

3. In libraries and on the Internet there are mountains of information. Paul says we find "all the hidden treasures of wisdom and knowledge" in Christ (v. 3). How might Paul understand the difference between information on the one hand, and wisdom and knowledge on the other?

*info. is no good w/out wisdom + knowledge W+K come only from God*

Nobody, no matter how learned or devout, could have guessed that when the one true God unveiled his blueprint for bringing the whole world under his sovereign and saving rule, that blueprint would consist of a man suffering the cruel punishment that the Romans used for rebel slaves and revolutionary leaders—and then rising from the dead three days later. But once these astonishing events had unfolded, Paul and others came to see that this map did indeed make sense. The treasure that was hidden, to which the map would lead them, was Jesus Christ himself.

4. Paul didn't see the human plight like so many do today, that people need to have some kind of spiritual experience and that Jesus the Messiah could supply it if they wanted. It was that King Jesus himself was the center of the cosmos, the key to life and the universe, the image of the invisible God, the clue to genuinely human existence.

Have you had difficulties with the idea that Jesus Christ is not one alternative way to have a spiritual experience but is the center of reality? Explain. *Not really. Questioned how Jesus dying saved, but not only way.*

5. If the centrality of Christ has not been a problem for you, why do you think other people find it offensive?
*So much of life is open to multiple options.*

6. Paul indicates that people are quite likely to try to deceive the new Christians with arguments that sound plausible but are in fact designed to lead them astray. What would protect the Colossians from these lies (vv. 2-5)?
*- Strong community w/ other believers*
*- Knowing Christ*

7.  What are some of today's "plausible words" which can deceive Christians?

- Bible's not trust worthy
- God didn't create
- God wouldn't allow suffering.

8.  Have you ever been fooled or at least enticed by plausible-sounding lies about Christian living? If so, what was the outcome? If not, how did you discern the falsehood?

Paul is anxious, since he can't be personally present with the little churches, that they should be able to line themselves up in battle array against any attack. The "good order" and "solidity" he speaks of (v. 5) would probably sound like military formation and readiness to defend. They mustn't be caught off their guard.

9.  In verses 6-7 Paul uses the three word-pictures of a journey, putting down healthy roots and a building being built. What do the three have in common?

10. How have you found your life in Christ to resemble

    a journey?

    developing healthy roots?

a building under construction?

11. In what areas of your life do you especially need the "wisdom and knowledge" of Christ?

## PRAY

Reread Colossians 2:2. Pray that the qualities Paul longed to see in the lives of the Colossians will also be apparent in you.

# COMPLETE IN CHRIST

*Colossians 2:8—3:4*

In Galatia, Jewish zealots had likely told the new converts that in becoming Christians they had only got half of what they needed. What
they now ought to do, to complete the experience, was to be circumcised
and to keep the law of Moses. Paul spent the whole of his letter to the
Galatians arguing that this was a complete misunderstanding, and that
to go this route would land the young Christians in real trouble. They
would be buying into a system which wouldn't do them any more good
than the paganism they had just left behind.

Colossae wasn't that far from Galatia, and now Paul is anxious that
similar people would come to the little church there with the same dan-
gerous message. Most towns or districts had a synagogue and at least
a small Jewish community. Don't get drawn into it, he says. It will be a
form of captivity for you.

### OPEN

How do you go about deciding what's true or not?

discernment, ~~God~~ God's word

STUDY

1. *Read Colossians 2:8—3:4.* Paul begins this part of his letter with one of the most important points in all of Christianity from that day to this. Jesus, he says, was and is not simply a fully human being (though he is) and not simply a man remarkably full of God (though he's that as well). He isn't a demigod, half divine and half human. What does Paul say about the identity of Jesus (vv. 2:9-10)?

*all of both God + Man*

2. Whatever new idea someone comes up with, Paul says, this is the acid test: Is it "in line with the king" (v. 2:8)? Does it have Jesus, the Messiah, the Lord, as its center and focus? If not, beware. What practical steps can a Christian take to "watch out" (v. 2:8) and not be captured by false ideas? *go to Gospels*

3. The practice Paul warns against in particular in 2:11-12 is circumcision. Why does he say it is not needed in addition to Christ?

*- Cross does it all*
*- heart was changed*

4. In circumcision, "putting off" a small piece of human flesh is trivial by comparison to "putting off" an entire way of life, an entire sphere of existence. This we did when we were baptized, Paul says, the mode and sign of entry into the Christian community from the earliest days to the present. In the last study we considered ways people believe Christ is not central. Here Paul argues against those who say that while Christ is perfectly fine, we just need to add

some other bit to make our spiritual life truly complete.

✳ What ideas or practices have you encountered that suggest we need to add something to our faith besides Jesus to make us "true" or "total" Christians? *Baptism, Rituals,*

5. How would Paul argue against those who suggest such things?

*- just like circumsion, we dont need other things.*
*- nailed to the cross w/ Him*

6. The "handwriting that was against us" (2:14) refers to the Jewish law, the law of Moses, which prevented Gentiles like the Colossians from getting into God's people and condemned Jews for breaking its commands.

How has God dealt with the condemnation of the law?

*- nailed to the cross*
*- things don't matter anymore*

7. For the Romans every crucifixion of a rebel king, even a strange one like Jesus, was another symbolic triumph for Rome, and hence, in Jewish eyes, for the power of paganism as a whole. Now blink, rub your eyes and read 2:14-15 again. On the cross, Paul declares, *God* was celebrating *his* triumph over the principalities and powers, the very powers that thought it was the other way around. Paul never gets tired of relishing the glorious paradox of the cross: God's weakness overcoming human strength, God's folly overcoming human wisdom.

Therefore, how in 2:16-19 does Paul say we should respond when people try to entice us with particular styles of piety or devotion other than single-minded devotion to Jesus?

There's nothing wrong with finding out what methods of prayer suit you best. But what Paul is talking about here is a system imposed by a certain sort of teacher, who goes on and on about visions he or she has had, living in a fantasy world in which only that one type of spiritual experience really "counts." Such people—and they're as frequent in the modern world as in the ancient—may then try to disqualify, or rule out of order, others who haven't had their type of experience, or who don't agree with their type of teaching.

8. When Paul mentions observing certain religious days or the regulations, "don't handle, don't taste, don't touch" certain things (2:16, 21), he is focusing attention on the appeal to pagans of Judaism's high moral code and heavy demands, a kind of religious fundamentalism.

Why does religious fundamentalism in today's hypermodern world have such appeal to different people around the globe?

-black+ white, not gray
-follow rules

9. Often when people are sick and tired of the murky, immoral world, they are glad to embrace a way of life which offers clear, bright, clean lines. Why, according to Paul, may these "give an appearance of wisdom" (2:23) but not actually be wise?

In 2:20-23, why does Paul characterize the "fundamentalist" behavior as worldly (see v. 20)?

10. By contrast, what characterizes the life of the spiritual person (vv. 3:1-4)? Live your life for Jesus . . .
not rules! Things that Matter!
• motivation

11. We who died with the Messiah don't belong to the old world any more. The regulations that are relevant there aren't relevant for us. We who were raised with the Messiah possess a true life in God's new world, the upper or heavenly world. That's where the real "me" is now to be found, "hidden with the king, in God" (v. 3:3).

Paul contrasts rules and regulations about what will disappear (2:22) with being "raised to life with the king" which "will be revealed with him in glory" (3:1-4). How is this contrast a helpful guide to discerning ways to live a holy life?

accountability

**PRAY**

Celebrate the completeness you have in Christ, who is God in all his fullness. Pray for discernment to recognize false teachers who try to impose a need for anything in addition to Christ.

Thank God that your life is safe in him. Pray that you will live daily with your focus on things that are above so that you will have a sure guide to how to live here and now.

**\*Prayer Requests:**

- Laura - co-workers daughter in ICU (car wreck)
- Landon - Student, Dale, infection
- Petrunins - baby coming! Alex
- Kris - guys @ work - apathy in dept.
- Seth & Mary - 2 kids maybe
  - Joe moving to Houston (Mary's Bro)!

THE FATHER SENT HIS ONLY SON
TO USHER IN HIS KINGDOM COME        INTRODUCE
TO TEACH THE WORLD OF HOPE AND ~~LOVE~~ PEACE
TO ~~TEACH OUR~~ WOUNDS, TO HEAL THE LEAST
LOVE AND JUSTICE COINCIDE
WHEN ON THE CROSS YOU CHOSE TO DIE
DEATH ~~HELL~~ AND HELL COULD NEVER HOLD YOU DOWN

AND THEN YOU GAVE ANOTHER ONE
WHEN FIRE FELL, THEY SPOKE IN TONGUES
THIS MYSTERY HAS US UNDONE
THAT GREATER THINGS WERE STILL TO COME

CHRIST IN ME
CHRIST IN ME
CRIST IN ME THE HOPE OF GLORY

@Durhams — Gentiels lead + feed

# OLD CLOTHES, NEW CLOTHES

*Colossians 3:5-17*

In the early church it was frequently the case that a candidate for baptism would take off the old suit of clothes they were wearing and then, after coming up from immersion, would be given a new set of clothes to wear. The new clothes would be white to signify the purity of the new life they were now entering. Paul knew that the young church in Colossae needed to know very clearly what was involved in putting off the old suit of clothes and putting on the new one. Certain patterns of behavior are the common coin of the world that remains ignorant of the God revealed in Jesus. Like a suit of clothes that's inappropriate for the occasion, these must be taken off, and the new patterns of behavior must be put on in their place.

## OPEN

When have you been in a situation in which you discovered that what you were wearing was inappropriate to the occasion? How did you try to explain your attire? What did you try to do about it?

## STUDY

1. *Read Colossians 3:5-17.* Suppose there was a business in which everybody behaved in the way described in verses 5-9. Suppose, a few miles down the road, there was another business where everybody behaved in the way described in verses 12-17. Which one would you rather work in, and why?


2. Why do you think some people would prefer to work in a business that is characterized by the description in verses 5-9?


3. Paul names two main areas of behavior as typical of the old lifestyle that is now to be abandoned. They have to do with sex on the one hand and speech on the other—two central areas of human life, both involving great potential for good and also for evil. Even though some pretend that such things are purely private matters, how does wrongdoing in these two areas of life lead to problems for a community as a whole?


4. What is the great transformation which Paul gives as the reason for our changed behavior (vv. 9-10)?

One result of new life in Christ is *new knowledge* (v. 10). Paul expects the Christian, as part of his or her renewal in the image of God—in other words, part of their discovery in practice of what it means to be a genuine human being—to be able to see clearly, and understand, the deeper issues involved behind apparently casual sexual behavior and apparently casual talk. Contrary to what a lot of people today imagine, being a Christian means learning to think harder, not to leave your brain behind in the quest for new experiences. Thinking straight and knowing the truth are part of what it means to be a truly human being, the sort of human being the gospel is meant to create.

5. In verses 10-11, Paul says that as a result of "being renewed in the image of the creator," old divisions of race, ethnicity, culture or geography must be done away with. In what ways might your Christian community exhibit this truth that Christ is "everything and in everything"?

6. Consider the behavior Paul sets forth in verses 12-17. Cynics might say that this is the behavior of weak-willed, wimpish people who cannot stand up for themselves. How would you respond to that charge about the difficulty of doing the things mentioned here like forgiving, being patient, being humble?

7. Being *tenderhearted* doesn't mean being sentimental. Being *kind* doesn't mean being a soft touch. *Humility* isn't the same thing as low self-esteem. *Meekness* is not weakness. How might you instead define each character trait?

How is a foundation of strength and confidence in Christ's peace the deciding factor in each?

8. Paul balances the negatives of the old life of sin with the positives of the new life in Christ. What is lacking when a Christian community denounces those things which should be "put off" without the corresponding emphasis on those things which should be "put on"?

9. A church with no (obvious) sexual sin but which is full of malicious gossip has only swapped one evil for another. Equally, a church where everyone is very caring and supportive but where immorality flourishes unchecked (perhaps precisely because people are afraid to confront it in case they're told they are being "unloving") is allowing noxious weeds to grow all around the flowers in the garden. You can't select some parts of the picture and leave others. For any of the parts to make sense, they all need to be in place.

Verse 16 portrays believers as teaching one another, exhorting (insistently encouraging) one another and singing to God with grateful hearts. How does your own Christian fellowship practice each of the three?

10. How can you contribute to the practice of each in your fellowship?

11. What key truth and key application are you taking from this passage?

Notice how Paul draws the picture together, again and again, with reference to the Lord, the king, Jesus himself. Jesus forgave you, so you must forgive. King Jesus is to be the decider in all your deliberations. His word is to be alive within the Christian community. And, finally, whatever you do or say must be able to stand having these words written above it: *In the name of the Lord Jesus.* Settle that in your hearts and minds and a great deal else will fall into place.

### PRAY

Ask the Holy Spirit to remove anything in your life which needs to be removed, and to increasingly clothe you with Christlikeness.

# THE CHRISTIAN HOUSEHOLD

*Colossians 3:18—4:1*

Freedom of choice" is one of the idols of our time. The suggestion of regulating or curtailing it is unthinkable for many people. But short-term freedom may lead to long-term captivity—slavery to chaos, injury and death. What proponents of absolute freedom fail to realize is that every exercise of supposed free choice severely limits all subsequent freedoms. The freedom of drivers to drive all over the road without looking just won't work over the long haul. We still need some Rules of the Road. One short "free" drive down the wrong side of the road could stop you ever being free to drive anywhere again. What Paul is offering in this passage of Scripture is a very brief Rules of the Road for household relationships.

## OPEN

What are some good things family members can do for each other? What are some harmful things?

## STUDY

1. *Read Colossians 3:18—4:1.* What's your initial overall reaction to this passage?

2. What questions does this passage raise for you?

3. In 3:18-21 what are the underlying attitudes in how family members are to treat one another?

4. How do Paul's commands to wives and to husbands complement one another (3:18-19)?

5. Paul's command to wives has come in for particular criticism. While I think verse 18 is best translated as "treat your husbands with respect," in many translations the key word in verse 18 comes out as *submit.* This conjures up the image of a downtrodden woman, the victim of her husband's every whim, unable to be herself, to think her own thoughts, to make a grown-up contribution to the relationship.

   What indications are there in this passage that this "downtrodden" image is not at all what Paul has in mind?

6.  What responsibilities do children and fathers have (3:20-21)?

    If each lived up to these, what would the resulting relationship look like?

7.  How does belonging to Christ the Master make a difference in how slaves work for their earthly masters (3:22-25)?

8.  How does belonging to Christ the Master make a difference in how earthly masters are to treat their slaves (4:1)?

9.  In Paul's day husbands and masters could rule supreme and unquestioned. (As we will see in the letter to Philemon at the end of this guide, Paul goes beyond this to make a revolutionary suggestion that a slave be freed.) How are Paul's Rules of the Road for relationships every bit as revolutionary as what some people might wish he had said?

10. What principles might employers and employees draw out of verses 3:22—4:1?

11. Paul offers only very brief guidelines about various relationships, and so he must have intended his audience to work out the details for themselves. It is no bad thing, then, for us today to do the same. What different (but equally legitimate and biblical) ways of raising a family or relating to coworkers can you think of?

12. Paul's code for household relationships is remarkable for several reasons. Paul's own fellow-workers included women and married couples, where it appears the women were, in our phrase, people in their own right. He doesn't just tell wives, children and slaves how to behave (as many pagan moralists of his day would have done). Their duties are balanced by the corresponding duties of husbands, parents and masters.

Whether in your family or work context, how can you grow and change in how you treat other believers?

## PRAY

Pray for Christian families who are under so much pressure to conform to the world's idea of freedom.

# 7

## TOGETHER IN PRAYER

*Colossians 4:2-18*

The best teachers make sure they get their pupils to take on some responsibility of their own. Most people, from quite small children upward, are ready to rise to the occasion if asked to do something on their own account. As long as the request is made in the right way, people are glad to be valued sufficiently to be entrusted with responsibility. That is what is going on in this passage from Colossians. Paul is the great apostle who has preached the gospel and planted churches halfway around the northern Mediterranean. The Colossians are new Christians who are taking their early steps in the faith. Yet he asks *them* to pray for *him*.

### OPEN

Is it easy or difficult for you to ask people to pray for you, and why?

How do you determine who you should ask to pray for you?

## STUDY

1. *Read Colossians 4:2-6.* Why does Paul feel a special need for the Colossians' prayers at this time?

2. What does it reveal about Paul that he asks the new Christians in Colossae to pray for him?

3. Having begun the letter by telling the Colossians that he is thanking God for them and praying for them, Paul now draws toward a close by asking them to do the same for him. No matter how senior or respected anyone is in the service of the gospel, they still need the prayers of the most apparently junior, humble and insignificant Christian. (I am speaking from a thoroughly earthly perspective; in God's eyes no Christian is more or less senior or junior, significant or insignificant, than any other.)

   Paul knows that he can talk all he likes, but unless God opens a door for the word to go through—the door, we assume, that lets the word into the hearts and lives of individuals and into the places where wider community issues are thrashed out—he will simply be making a useless noise. The door doesn't open automatically. What opens that door, again and again, is prayer.

   When have you seen a door open for you in response to the prayers of other Christians (v. 3)?

4. Why is it so important for us to "speak clearly" about the gospel (v. 4)?

5. What are the situations in your life where you need vigilance to "behave wisely towards outsiders," that is, people who have not come under the reign of Jesus (v. 5)?

6. The Colossians must learn to speak with "grace" and "salt" (v. 6), presumably meaning that whatever else they do, they mustn't be boring! And they must use every opportunity to do so (v. 5), becoming skilled in the art of real listening to the questions and comments made by puzzled onlookers and being sure they answer the person appropriately, rather than just parroting stock responses.

   List some ways that we might put verses 5-6 into practice in our everyday living.

7. The Colossians have never seen Paul face to face, but once you have prayed for someone, and once you realize they are praying for you as well, a bond grows up which creates a relationship of love and trust ahead of any personal contact. We are often asked to pray for people we have never met and probably never will meet, such as missionaries in other countries, victims of disasters thousands of miles away, or relatives and friends of people in our church.

What keeps you praying for those people even though you don't know them?

8. *Read Colossians 4:7-18.* As Paul concludes his letter he conveys greetings to or from almost a dozen people, not counting an indefinite number at Laodicea and the church in Nympha's house.

   What is the common thread which stitches all these people together?

9. From this collection of greetings at the close of his letter, what do you sense about Paul's personality?

10. Paul's own vulnerability emerges in his remarks about Aristarchus, Mark and Jesus Justus. Paul had been violently opposed by his fellow Jews wherever he had gone—not that he would have been surprised, because that had been his own reaction to the gospel before his conversion. These three colleagues are his only fellow-workers who are also Jewish. It is a comfort to him. Paul was not, as people often make out, an arrogant man, smug in his own rightness. He was deeply human, and this mention of one comfort of this sort reminds us just how many conflicting emotions he must have had to cope with, living the life he did and facing new challenges and dangers every day.

At difficult times in your Christian life, how have fellow Christians been a particular comfort and support to you?

11. In this letter Paul shows himself to be a great thinker about who Christ is and what he has done. He also shows himself to be a pastor and friend in Christ. The question is whether we in our day can hold together the thinking and writing of great thoughts and the challenge of pastoral care, prayer and concern.

    If a church emphasizes personal care but de-emphasizes teaching, what may be the result?

    If a church emphasizes teaching but de-emphasizes personal care, what may be the result?

12. How does the entire closing of Paul's letter (vv. 7-18) speak to individual Christians who feel they can go it alone and have nothing to gain or learn from other Christians and churches?

**PRAY**

The point Paul is making throughout his letter to the Colossians is the thousand ways in which Christians belong to one another in a fellowship of mutual love, prayer, instruction and service. Pray that the Lord will stitch your fellowship together in love and also that he will stitch you together with believers in Christ's church worldwide.

# GRACIOUS PERSUASION

*Philemon*

Persuasion, particularly the persuasion that comes genuinely "in the Lord," is a remarkable thing. Of course it can be misrepresented: as manipulation, as bullying, as unfair pressure. All those things do exist, and they're ugly. Often people who don't like the eventual decision are tempted to say that the persuasion they received comes into one of those categories.

But there is a subtle and delicate interplay between explaining something in genuine love, with a true vision of the gospel, and someone else making up their mind in the light of it. To avoid all attempts to persuade, to encourage, to show people things in a new light, because you're frightened of the accusation of being manipulative, would leave us all free—but only "free" to be hermits, bereft of all human contact.

Paul knew the dangers of trying to force someone to do something. His style throughout the letter to Philemon is one of gentle, almost playful, Christian persuasion.

## OPEN

Recall a time when you played the role of a reconciler, approaching someone on behalf of another person. What were your hopes? What were your fears? How did you decide what approach to take?

Or, if you'd rather, recall a time when someone approached you on behalf of another person. What did you think at first? What made the person persuasive or not persuasive? How did you respond?

## STUDY

1. *Read Philemon 1-7.* Philemon lived in Colossae and had apparently become a Christian through hearing Paul preach. Like every person of any substance in that world, Philemon owned slaves. One of them, Onesimus ("Useful"), had run away, which was a capital offense. Worse, the slave had probably helped himself to some money as he left. Onesimus had come under Paul's influence and had become a Christian. He and Paul had become friends, brothers in the Lord Jesus, close partners in the gospel. Now Paul was going to make huge demands on both Onesimus and Philemon; he was going to send Onesimus back to Philemon and ask Philemon to accept him back again without penalty—and perhaps even hint that Onesimus should be set free.

   How would you describe the mood of these opening paragraphs of Paul's letter?

2. What can you tell about the quality of Paul's relationships with the various people mentioned?

3. When Paul tells people what he's praying for when he thinks of them, this often gives us the clue to the inner meaning of the letter. What is Paul praying for Philemon, and what could his prayer have to do with the matter of Onesimus?

Paul is praying that the partnership which he and Philemon share in the gospel will be productive and will have the effect it's meant to have. They are, as it were, in business together and must be loyal colleagues. When people believe the gospel, they are brought into partnership with all others who believe it. This partnership must have its powerful effect. The effect will be in realizing every good thing that is at work in them. *Realizing* means not only *recognizing and knowing* but also *putting into practice*. The gospel itself is at work in Christians by the power of God's Spirit. As it does its work, it produces new things, good things, new ways of living for individuals, households and communities.

4. *Read Philemon 8-14.* How does Paul give his own stamp of approval to and identify with Onesimus?

5. How else does Paul seek to persuade Philemon while still showing respect to him?

Paul's appeal is one of love. Having established that he and Philemon are bonded together with strands of love, partnership, affection and respect, Paul is now going to show that he and Onesimus have established a similar bond. When to his surprise Philemon discovers that his runaway slave has returned, Paul doesn't want him just to see Onesimus standing there. He wants Philemon to see Paul himself. This is the heart of Paul's strategy in this delicate and highly skillful piece of writing. Would that all Christian persuaders could learn from it.

6. *Read Philemon 15-25.* How does Paul draw Philemon's attention to the larger purposes of God?

7. When has an apparent loss led you to recognize God at work?

8. What is Christlike about what Paul offers to do in verses 17-20?

9. The gospel is not simply a message about how people "get saved" in a purely spiritual way. It's about the lordship of Jesus the king over the real world, over people's real lives, over the difficult decisions that real people face. The letter of Philemon is a living example of the Christian practice of reconciliation, not only of reconciling us with God but of us with each other.

In your world (church, family, workplace, community) where does reconciliation need to happen?

10. What first step could you and others who believe in Jesus take in that direction, and (as with Paul) what might the cost be?

11. What guidance does the letter of Philemon offer for making appeals for reconciliation?

## PRAY

Pray about situations in which you must make a difficult appeal, or appeal to a difficult person. Pray that your appeal will be made in the love and wisdom of Christ.

# Guidelines for Leaders

*My grace is sufficient for you.*
*(2 Corinthians 12:9)*

If leading a small group is something new for you, don't worry. These sessions are designed to flow naturally and be led easily. You may even find that the studies seem to lead themselves!

This study guide is flexible. You can use it with a variety of groups—students, professionals, coworkers, friends, neighborhood or church groups. Each study takes forty-five to sixty minutes in a group setting.

You don't need to be an expert on the Bible or a trained teacher to lead a small group. These guides are designed to facilitate a group's discussion, not a leader's presentation. Guiding group members to discover together what the Bible has to say and to listen together for God's guidance will help them remember much more than a lecture would.

There are some important facts to know about group dynamics and encouraging discussion. The suggestions listed below should equip you to effectively and enjoyably fulfill your role as leader.

## PREPARING FOR THE STUDY

1. Ask God to help you understand and apply the passage in your own life. Unless this happens, you will not be prepared to lead others. Pray too for the various members of the group. Ask God to open

your hearts to the message of his Word and motivate you to action.

2. Read the introduction to the entire guide to get an overview of the topics that will be explored.

3. As you begin each study, read and reread the assigned Bible passage to familiarize yourself with it. This study guide is based on the For Everyone series on the New Testament (published by SPCK and Westminster John Knox). It will help you and the group if you have on hand a copy of the companion volume from the For Everyone series both for the translation of the passage found there and for further insight into the passage.

4. Carefully work through each question in the study. Spend time in meditation and reflection as you consider how to respond.

5. Write your thoughts and responses in the space provided in the study guide. This will help you to express your understanding of the passage clearly.

6. It may help to have a Bible dictionary handy. Use it to look up any unfamiliar words, names or places. The glossary at the end of each New Testament for Everyone commentary may likewise be helpful for keeping discussion moving.

7. Reflect seriously on how you need to apply the Scripture to your life. Remember that the group members will follow your lead in responding to the studies. They will not go any deeper than you do.

## LEADING THE STUDY

1. At the beginning of your first time together, explain that these studies are meant to be discussions, not lectures. Encourage the members of the group to participate. However, do not put pressure on those who may be hesitant to speak—especially during the first few sessions.

2. Be sure that everyone in your group has a study guide. Encourage the group to prepare beforehand for each discussion by reading the introduction to the guide and by working through the questions in each study.

3. Begin each study on time. Open with prayer, asking God to help the group to understand and apply the passage.

4. Have a group member read aloud the introduction at the beginning of the discussion.

5. Discuss the "Open" question before the Bible passage is read. The "Open" question introduces the theme of the study and helps group members to begin to open up, and can reveal where our thoughts and feelings need to be transformed by Scripture. Reading the passage first will tend to color the honest reactions people would otherwise give—because they are, of course, supposed to think the way the Bible does. Encourage as many members as possible to respond to the "Open" question, and be ready to get the discussion going with your own response.

6. Have a group member read aloud the passage to be studied as indicated in the guide.

7. The study questions are designed to be read aloud just as they are written. You may, however, prefer to express them in your own words.

   There may be times when it is appropriate to deviate from the study guide. For example, a question may have already been answered. If so, move on to the next question. Or someone may raise an important question not covered in the guide. Take time to discuss it, but try to keep the group from going off on tangents.

8. Avoid answering your own questions. An eager group quickly becomes passive and silent if members think the leader will do most of the talking. If necessary repeat or rephrase the question until it is clearly understood, or refer to the commentary woven into the guide to clarify the context or meaning.

9. Don't be afraid of silence in response to the discussion questions. People may need time to think about the question before formulating their answers.

10. Don't be content with just one answer. Ask, "What do the rest of you think?" or "Anything else?" until several people have given answers to the question.

11. Try to be affirming whenever possible. Affirm participation. Never reject an answer; if it is clearly off-base, ask, "Which verse led you to that conclusion?" or again, "What do the rest of you think?"

12. Don't expect every answer to be addressed to you, even though this will probably happen at first. As group members become more at ease, they will begin to truly interact with each other. This is one sign of healthy discussion.

13. Don't be afraid of controversy. It can be very stimulating. If you don't resolve an issue completely, don't be frustrated. Explain that the group will move on and God may enlighten all of you in later sessions.

14. Periodically summarize what the group has said about the passage. This helps to draw together the various ideas mentioned and gives continuity to the study. But don't preach.

15. Conclude your time together with the prayer suggestion at the end of the study, adapting it to your group's particular needs as appropriate. Ask for God's help in following through on the applications you've identified.

16. End on time.

Many more suggestions and helps for studying a passage or guiding discussion can be found in *How to Lead a LifeGuide Bible Study* and *The Big Book on Small Groups* (both from InterVarsity Press/USA).

# Other InterVarsity Press Resources from N. T. Wright

*The Challenge of Jesus*
N. T. Wright offers clarity and a full accounting of the facts of the life and teachings of Jesus, revealing how the Son of God was also solidly planted in first-century Palestine. *978-0-8308-2200-3, 202 pages, hardcover*

*Resurrection*
This 50-minute DVD confronts the most startling claim of Christianity—that Jesus rose from the dead. Shot on location in Israel, Greece and England, N. T. Wright presents the political, historical and theological issues of Jesus' day and today regarding this claim. Wright brings clarity and insight to one of the most profound mysteries in human history. Study guide included.
*978-0-8308-3435-8, DVD*

*Evil and the Justice of God*
N. T. Wright explores all aspects of evil and how it presents itself in society today. Fully grounded in the story of the Old and New Testaments, this presentation is provocative and hopeful; a fascinating analysis of and response to the fundamental question of evil and justice that faces believers.
*978-0-8308-3398-6, 176 pages, hardcover*

*Evil*
Filmed in Israel, South Africa and England, this 50-minute DVD confronts some of the major "evil" issues of our time—from tsunamis to AIDS—and puts them under the biblical spotlight. N. T. Wright says there is a solution to the problem of evil, if only we have the honesty and courage to name it and understand it for what it is. Study guide included. *978-0-8308-3434-1, DVD*

*Justification: God's Plan and Paul's Vision*
In this comprehensive account and defense of the crucial doctrine of justification, Wright also responds to critics who have challenged what has come to be called the new perspective. Ultimately, he provides a chance for those in the middle of and on both sides of the debate to interact directly with his views and form their own conclusions. *978-0-8308-3863-9, 279 pages, hardcover*

*Colossians and Philemon*
In Colossians, Paul presents Christ as "the firstborn over all creation," and appeals to his readers to seek a maturity found only Christ. In Philemon, Paul appeals to a fellow believer to receive a runaway slave in love and forgiveness. In this volume N. T. Wright offers comment on both of these important books.
*978-0-8308-4242-1, 199 pages, paperback*